# Proportion In Gothic Architecture

# Philip Freeman

# PROPORTION

IN

# GOTHIC ARCHITECTURE.

## A PAPER,

READ AT A MEETING OF

### The Cambridge Architectural Society,

MARCH 3, 1848.

---

BY

## THE REV. PHILIP FREEMAN, M.A.

LATE FELLOW OF SAINT PETER'S COLLEGE, CAMBRIDGE;
PRINCIPAL OF THE DIOCESAN COLLEGE, CHICHESTER.

CAMBRIDGE:
Published for the Society,
BY MESSRS J. & J. J. DEIGHTON,
MACMILLAN, BARCLAY & CO., & E. MEADOWS.
LONDON: J. MASTERS. OXFORD: J. H. PARKER.

1848.

# ON PROPORTION

## IN

# GOTHIC ARCHITECTURE.

THE object of this paper is to bring under the notice of the Society one of the most remarkable discoveries of modern architectural science, and to investigate the principles which appear to be involved in it. Various attempts have, at different times, been made to ascertain the rules by which the architects of the middle ages were guided in determining the proportions and arrangement of their buildings, but hitherto with but little success. The rules propounded have generally been of too partial or uncertain application to command our assent to them; or indeed to solve, in a satisfactory manner, the phenomenon which they profess to account for. Some of these theories will be alluded to hereafter.

The discovery I speak of has been given to the world by Mr Griffith, in his work entitled, "Ancient Gothic Churches, their Proportions and Chromatics[1]." He has shewn that the ground-plan, and in a great measure the other arrangements, of Gothic buildings, are based upon regular geometrical figures, chiefly the equilateral triangle, though sometimes also the square. The specimens exhibited, copied by Mr Griffith's kind permission, will give the best idea of the system. No. 1. is the

[1] Published by the author, 9 St John's-square, London; printed by Gilbert and Rivington.

ground-plan of the Church of the Holy Sepulchre, Cambridge. If in the interior circumference of the building two squares, alternating with each other, be described, and, within these again, two other squares, the intersections of the two last-mentioned squares will give the centres of the eight columns; the angles of the two larger squares marking the position of the doorway and windows. The same is the case at S. Sepulchre's, Northampton. No. 2. exhibits the ground-plan of Little Maplested Church, Essex. If an equilateral triangle be inscribed within the circular or western part, with the apex at the centre of the western door,—and another triangle alternating with this,—the apices of the triangles will decide the centres of the four windows, and of the chancel-arch; while *the angles formed by the intersecting sides* decide the *position of the six pillars*, which are equi-triangular, with half-shafts attached to each face: and the radii passing through these intersections are the central lines of the buttresses. Again, if the double circle which circumscribes the western part, or nave, be repeated eastward, it will exactly circumscribe the eastern part, or chancel; while the points of the *alternating* equilateral triangles, inscribed as before, will decide the position of the windows and buttresses. There are two windows not accounted for by this means; but their position, and the *width* both of them and of all the other windows, is decided for us in another way; their place is in that part of the wall which intervenes between the circumferences of the touching circles. The bisection of the base of one of the triangles gives the centre of the apse. This must be allowed to be a very curious and beautiful specimen of arrangement. By way of illustration of it, I have added the ground-plan of the Church of S. Agnes at Rome, (formerly, it is supposed, the temple of Bacchus,) as it is given by Palladio (No. 3.) It will be seen that its twelve pairs of columns are in like manner regulated, as to position, by the intersection of the sides of *four* equilateral triangles, whose apices are arranged in the same manner round the building, and decide the position of the door-way and niches. No. 4. is still more remarkable. It exhibits the ground-plan of the Temple Church, London. Here the *external* circle, including the buttresses, is that which regulates the plan. In the nave, or circular part, the inscribed equilateral triangles decide not merely the position, but the *width*, of the windows; the *opening* of the west door, and of the chancel-arch, and the projection of the buttresses. A hexagon inscribed within the hexagon formed by the intersecting sides of the triangles, gives the position of the six pillars. A repetition of the circle and triangles eastward, (the circles touching,) decides the main features of the chancel, as follows:—four of the columns lie on the sides of the triangles, close to their intersections; two more on the transverse diameter of the circle. The transverse bases of the triangles fix the place of four of the buttresses; the transverse diameter that of two more: equidistance regulating the remaining pillars and buttresses. But a still more astonishing result of the application of the principle to this Church remains to be stated. No. 5. is a *section* of the chancel, to the same scale. It will be seen that the self-same equilateral triangle, which regulated the ground-plan, will, when set up on its transverse base, fix the position and pitch of the central roof, and so the whole interior height of the building. Let a circle be circumscribed about it, and the alternating triangle drawn. Its base decides the spring of the roof, or height of the walls from the ground: minor equilateral triangles erected upon this base give the gables of the aisles. The transverse diameter of the circle gives the height of the pillars: the centres of the arches are found by the intersections of various lines in the figure; finally, a square circumscribed about the circle decides the projections of the buttresses; and a concentric arc embraces the apices of the central and side roofs. Mr Griffith has applied the same test to the ground-plan and elevation of Malmsbury Abbey Church, and with the like remarkable results. I have myself applied it to the ground-plan and elevation of Hawton chancel, published on a large and accurate scale by the Cambridge Camden Society. It will be seen (No. 6.) that the bases of the equilateral triangles (they are measured from the middle of the walls) fix the position of the buttresses (south side) and of the door (north and south side), while the point of the eastern triangle gives the distance between the principal mullions of the east window. The points where the circles cut the walls decide the width of the side windows. The same triangle applied to the elevation, gives the height of the east window *jambs*, and that of the other window-*arch* : the east window-*arch* is one-third of the triangle higher. No. 7. is the ground-plan of King's College Chapel, from Mr Wilkins' measurement. Nothing can exceed the completeness and exactitude with which the application of the equilateral triangle accounts for all the dimensions and arrangements. The entire width of the Chapel, including the side-chapels between the buttresses, and measured from the middle of the external walls, being taken as a base; and alternating equilateral triangles being drawn as before; and a circle circumscribed; and the whole figure thrice repeated; the adjacent circles also touching:—*the intersections of the sides of the triangles* will give the breadth of the Chapel itself, including the thickness of the walls; the successive bases of the triangles fall in the middle (as it seems) of the alternate buttresses, the place of the intermediate ones being upon the transverse diameters of the circles. Moreover, if triangles be drawn alternating again with those already drawn, they will decide the dimensions of the buttresses. The eastern turrets come just within the sweep of the last circle, and the western within that of an additional circle intersecting the last circle westward : and a triangle within this circle decides the breadth of the western door. The width of the doorways and porches is also settled by the various intersections of the lines : and thus the whole of the features of the ground-plan are decided. Mr Griffith also assures us that he has applied the same test to the ground-plans of Westminster Abbey and York Minster; Salisbury, Ely, Winchester, and Rochester Cathedrals; Bath Abbey, and S. Mary, Redcliffe, with entire success. I have myself found it answer when applied to Chichester Cathedral, and S. Mary's, Taunton. He has also shewn that it applies to the *elevations* of S. Mary's, Oxford, and Henry VII.'s Chapel, Westminster; and is confident that it is of universal application, not only for ground-plans (as well of the minor features as of the entire structure), but also for fixing the height of the nave, its columns and roof, the centres of the arches, &c.

Such, then, is the discovery of Mr Griffith. And the first remark that I shall make upon it is, that it *is a* true, genuine, and unquestionable *discovery;* not a mere theory, but a *discovered truth.* It is the system, not of Des Cartes, but of Newton. I mean, that as far as

regards the buildings,—and they are pretty numerous,—
to which he has applied his principle, it may be considered
as *perfectly certain*, that the architects of those buildings
constructed them on the basis of the geometrical figures
here applied to them. Any man who believes that it is
the result of accident, or even of intuition,—of an intuitive perception of the correct and beautiful,—that the
Temple Church, for instance, or King's College Chapel,
are capable of being mapped out, as we have seen that
they may be, on the equi-laterali-triangular basis,—such a
man may as reasonably believe, with Epicurus and Lucre-
tius, that the universe was made by a fortuitous concourse
of atoms, or, with Wolf and his followers, that the Iliad
is a collection of unconnected ballads. With what truth
it may be said that these geometrical principles are applicable to all Gothic buildings whatsoever, is a question
which must be decided by a very wide induction from ex-
amples: and I would suggest it as a very worthy field of
study for this Society, to pursue the investigation with
reference to as many churches and cathedrals as possible.
This pursuit involves, of course, the necessity for accurate
plans and elevations; in many instances such have already
been made; but in many more they have yet to be constructed. A Sub-Committee might perhaps be appointed
with advantage, to receive and systematize information
on the subject, and give a direction to the researches of
the Members of the Society. The theory, if it can be
proved to possess *anything like universality*, *must* come to
have a most important influence on the erection of new
churches. And even without this,—should there not be
found one single church more to which the principle applies,—yet surely, even so, wise men will think there is a
greater chance of success in adopting the principles which

guided the erection of Westminster, and York, and Salisbury, and Ely, and S. Mary Redcliffe, and the Temple, and King's College Chapel, than in building, as hitherto, at random. It is highly reasonable to believe that this is the one great thing wanting to the success of our imitations of the middle age architecture, viz. the knowledge of their geometrical principles of arrangement: that this is the one indescribable *want*,—ever felt, but never accounted for,—which differences modern from ancient Pointed Architecture.

And I would just observe, that the adoption of such geometrical principles, carried out as it *was* carried out by the mediæval architects, far from cramping invention, and fettering genius, just furnishes the architect with welcome boundaries, and broad general suggestions and monitions, within which to exercise his art. Probably there is no modern architect that has sat down to plan a Gothic church, but has "felt the weight of too much liberty:" or who would not give worlds for some better reason for doing one thing in preference to another, than the mere caprice of his own taste, or the results of his own observation, however wide, can supply. We see that the equi-laterali-triangular basis, for instance, allows of infinite variety in its application; it only imposes a restrictive law within which all is freedom: it realises what Sir Francis Palgrave eulogises as the perfect state to live under, *subjecti libertas*—"the liberty of the subject." Such restrictions are what metre and rhyme are to the poet: he would not be without them, but rather, as Kirke White says, "hugs his chains."

It may be added, that this condition of *limited freedom* is exactly what meets us in those departments of Gothic Architecture which we are better acquainted with. It is analogous to that *prescript outline*, with infinitely varied detail, which pervades tracery, mouldings, and all kinds of ornamental features. Thus, *tracery* must be geometrical as to its principles of formation (a very exact analogy this to the case before us); curved *mouldings* must be worked in subordination to angular plan; *crockets* must be of a certain outline in each style respectively; *poppy-heads* must be of the fleur-de-lys form: but within these restrictions infinite variety has place.

But I have a further object in this paper, than that of directing attention to Mr Griffith's discovery, or recommending a more complete verification of it on the ground of its importance. I propose to investigate, as I said at the outset, more fully than he has done, the *principles* which appear to be involved in this theory. We see the mediæval architects planning and erecting their buildings with these geometrical figures as the basis of their arrangements. Can any reason be assigned for their doing so, beyond the obvious ones of convenience and regularity? That it is convenient, and more agreeable, to find oneself working on a plan than at random, has already been incidentally pointed out; and again, that regularity of any kind possesses a charm, as compared with utter lawlessness, in the matter of building, is no less evident. But does the *rationale* of the matter go any deeper than this? Is there any more *intimate* propriety than this, in the adoption of these geometrical figures as a basis? does a deep and true theory of the beautiful, in respect of proportion and arrangement, lie at the bottom of it? Our prepossessions in behalf of Pointed Architecture must surely lead us to expect that an affirmative reply can be made to this question. We acknowledge, on the one hand, an exquisite beauty, propriety, harmony, of various forms, kinds, and degrees, in these wonderful, and to us mysterious fabrics, the Cathedrals and Churches of the Middle Ages. And we discover, on the other hand, so as to be perfectly certain we *have* discovered it, the principle on which these buildings were arranged. We are not justified, it is true, in *assuming* that these two phenomena stand related to each other as cause and effect; but a very shrewd suspicion must arise that such is the case. The question is, how to connect the two phenomena. What reason can be given, why geometrical arrangement of any kind should produce architectural beauty in general: or why this particular kind of it should result in structures which affect the eye with such unrivalled impressions of beauty and harmony?

Now the subject of Proportion in general is one on which much has been written, but very little, it is humbly conceived, understood: it is generally left, at last, in a hazy indistinctness, the convenient refuge of ignorance. " Much of the beauty of architecture," observes one writer[1], " depends upon *proportion;* or, in other words, on that well balanced regulation of the different parts of a structure, which affects the eye and mind agreeably, all the members seeming agreeably adjusted to the whole...Accordingly, great stress has been laid upon proportion by architectural writers; yet what they have said respecting it amounts to little more than artistical jargon; e. g. they generally restrict the term to proportion, as regards individual parts....What is it," he proceeds, " if not the beautiful adjustment of parts to parts, that captivates us... in the productions of Gothic Architecture? or wherefore do some buildings in that style charm us so much more than

[1] Penny Cyclopædia, art. " Proportion."

others,...if not either by the harmony of their proportions, or the effect produced by some particular one, such as loftiness, &c.?...Far from being devoid of proportions, Gothic admits of infinitely greater variety in this respect than the classical styles; instead of being at all deficient in the elements and principles constituting proportion, it contains them in much greater abundance. It is indeed not the poverty, but the copiousness of the Gothic, as regards diversity of proportions, that renders it almost impossible to systematize it, and reduce it like the classic orders to a few positive rules, which may be learnt mechanically....As to the internal proportions of buildings, we shall only observe that beauty and harmony of proportions depend very much upon the particular purpose for which the building is intended. Whether an interior or exterior design, it is requisite that the individual features should be so well balanced and adjusted that the *ensemble* shall at once produce a pleasing impression upon the spectators; which kind of *eurhythmia*, or general harmony of proportions, admits of so many modifications, and depends so greatly upon the precise nature and character of the particular design, that direct precepts avail but little towards its attainment; on which account it must be acquired chiefly by taste, guided by study and observation." This is the writing of a man who really had nothing to say, and who conceals his want of meaning beneath that very artistical jargon which he sets out with deprecating. All that he does say amounts to this, that proportion is the proper adjustment of parts, and that the proper adjustments of parts is proportion. He does not furnish or suggest a single test or principle by which to judge whether a building is or is not well-proportioned. All is referred to a pleasing impression on the eye; but why such impression is produced by any one kind of arrangement rather than by another, is not explained.

· Nevertheless,—notwithstanding, that is, all the unmeaning jargon which has been talked on the subject,—(the above is one of the latest specimens, taken from one of the popular lights of the day), let us still not be discouraged from investigating the subject of PROPORTION. That there is such a thing, our senses or our judgment informs us. We pass judgment instinctively on *extreme* cases of disproportion: a room obviously too low for its size, or a tower palpably too tall for its bulk, offends the most unpractised eye. And the trained judgment and taste grows to an increased consciousness of preference for certain forms and dimensions which strike it as harmonious and graceful, over others which it condemns as unsightly. Now is this a mere matter of taste? Surely not. All men are more or less agreed upon these preferences. There must, therefore, be something in our nature, physical or metaphysical, to account for such agreement.

Let us first inquire how the *Greeks* treated architecture. Did they consider proportion entirely a matter of taste, or did they refer it to fixed principles? Now as no regular treatise of theirs has come down to us, we have no direct testimony to allege; but their mind is sufficiently declared by the name they gave to "harmony of construction." They called it, not ἁρμονία—not a quasi-musical *fitness*; nor even ἀναλογία, "the preservation of due relations," which is either a vague conception, or else a merely numerical one;—not these, but ΣΥΜΜΕΤΡΙΑ. The Latins rendered this word, as applied to architecture, in various ways; as the younger Pliny by *congruentia*, or *æqualitas*; Gellius by *commoditas*; Suetonius by *competentia*; Vitruvius by *commensus*. But Pliny the elder frankly confesses that the Latins had no synonyme for it.

"Symmetria Latinum nomen non habet[1]." Vitruvius, the only practical man among them all, admits as much by coining *commensus* as its rendering; and at the same time affirms thereby *his* view of the thing meant; namely, that it was the principle of "commeasurement," or "capability of being referred to one standard of measure." And this view he carried out in his architectural system. To him we may pass on, as the Roman reviver, in the days either of Julius and Augustus Cæsar, or of some later emperor, (v. Enc. Brit. p. 22.) of the Greek architecture.

The plan of his *renaissance* was to measure, foot by foot and inch by inch, the Greek models. . Taking the semi-diameter of the column as his *unit of measure*, (or as he called it, as the *module*) and dividing this into minutes and seconds, he formed a very complete system of *linear* measurement. Any part of a composition was described as being of so many modules, minutes, &c., in height, breadth, or projection. (Encycl. Brit.) But Vitruvius did not really understand Grecian architecture. He was the very prince of servile copyists: but he knew nothing of the great principles of proportion and arrangement acted on by the Greeks. He bestows but slight attention on superficial or internal proportion: his linear measurements apply, after all, only to columns and entablatures. It is even doubted whether he ever saw a Greek temple. It is said that "not a single example of Greek architecture will bear out a single rule which Vitruvius prescribes, professedly on its authority: that not an existing edifice, or fragment of an edifice, in form or proportion, is in perfect accordance with any law of that author, nor indeed are they generally referable to the principles which he lays down." (Encycl. Brit. p. 22.) In short,

---

[1] Plin. Lib. iv. 38.

it is pretty well agreed that Vitruvius was an arrant quack, his knowledge of *fact* being very slender and inaccurate, and his acquaintance with principles absolutely *nothing*. Only he *had* got a glimmering of this truth, *that architectural proportion is based in some way upon measurement*; and for the preservation of this truth we must feel indebted to him, faulty and worthless as was the entire theory in which he has embodied it.

We pass on to the second revival of classic architecture, in the 15th century, commonly known as the *cinquecento*, or the *renaissance*. The founder of this school was Brunelleschi; its most eminent scholars, perhaps, Alberti and Palladio. Vitruvius was translated, and became the text book of the revived science,—the Aristotle of these architectural schoolmen. Palladio and others published, moreover, delineations and admeasurements of Roman architectural remains in Italy; with, however, many inaccuracies and misrepresentations. (Ibid.) With their errors of execution we are not now concerned; but only with observing what their conception of ancient architecture was: and we see them, like Vitruvius, referring all proportion to actual measurement, not to fancy. In fact, they adopted the Vitruvian system wholesale, with such corrections in matters of detail as examination of models might furnish. And from hence that system in all its parts,—its minuteness in columnar measurement, and its laxity in proportion of every other kind, and on any larger scale,—has flowed down into the classico-architectural schools of modern Europe. It has been well observed of these (Penny Cyclop. art. " Proportion," p. 53.) that " though they insist upon the strictest regard to certain proportions as far as ' the order,' i. e. the columns and entablature alone are concerned, they make amends for such rigour by liberally tolerating the utmost laxity as to proportion in other respects. Provided 'the order' be of legitimate proportion in itself, it may be quite out of proportion to the whole of the structure." Of course, according as architects possessed more or less of intuitive genius, they produced better proportioned buildings in all respects : but such happier efforts are in no degree to be ascribed to the traditional architectural system, which made no provision for proportions, beyond the meagre code of rules we have been speaking of.

Leaving now Vitruvius, and the attempted revivals of Classical architecture, we come to such attempts as have been made to investigate the principles of proportion which guided the mediæval architects. The field is not large. It is unnecessary to say that whatever has been attempted in this way, is of very recent date : as it is only of late years that Gothic architecture has excited anything like intelligent and admiring inquiry. A paper was read, I believe, not long since, before the Oxford Architectural Society, in which the endeavour was made to establish some canons as to the proportions of Chancels. And similar partial and desultory essays have perhaps been made in other quarters[1]. But I am not aware of any other publications on the subject, than those of Mr Billings and Mr Wallen ; — the former, in his "Attempt to define the Geometric proportions of Gothic architecture;" the latter, in a paper read before the Yorkshire Polytechnic Society. Both these works are referred to, and their substance stated, in an interesting and ingenious article, " On the Philosophy of Gothic Architecture," in No. IV. (Dec. 1844) of the English Review. It is well observed there, that we owe a debt to those writers

[1] Vid. Creasy on Engineering.

" for having boldly asserted the great principle, that the works of Gothic art are not a chance or fanciful congeries, but *are constructed in all their details upon some fixed and profound law.*" It is one thing, however, to assert this, and even to bring convincing reasons for believing it to be so; which I think these writers have succeeded in doing: and quite another to be able to enunciate the law or principle in question; which I am equally of opinion they have failed to do.

Mr Wallen's hypothesis, e. g., about the interval and elevation at which pointed arches should be placed in a building, is "that the segments of circles occurring in Gothic architecture ought, if prolonged and completed, to fall one within another as far as possible, and pass through other lines of the building at some regular point of intersection, dividing them into some equal or proportionate limbs. Thus the curve of a window, on the exterior, should sweep round, touching some leading line, or some point marked by a prominent corbel, &c. Thus the arches of the nave should, if the circles were completed, form intersecting colonnades, &c." This is an elegant theory, and probably has something in it; but as a whole it is surely fanciful. The rule, e. g. about the window-arches is so lax, as not to be much of a test; that about the nave arches *is an impossibility*, except *where the arches are equilateral or acute.* In obtuse arches it is clear that the curve of the arch, if carried round, will fall upon the diameter too soon to embrace a second similar arch. And at best, were the theory strictly true and universally applicable, its field is, after all, very limited. A part of the theory more worthy of our attention, is that which endeavours to account for the proportions of Gothic ground-plans.

2

With reference to this, the Reviewer already quoted remarks, p. 404, that "there is one branch of the philosophy of Gothic architecture, which hitherto has been little studied, and still less applied to practice: viz., the laws [*sic legend. pro*, "in the laws"] of geometrical proportion observed by ancient architects." Further on he speaks of those "immutable laws of the human mind, to which, and not to mere capricious arbitrary fancies, the great architects of old conformed, in the creation of beauty: and without which we shall neither be able to reach the real laws of ancient art in their highest generalizations, nor to criticise its works by any fixed standard, nor to imitate without incongruities. That there *is* a law of proportion to be observed, even in the most varied forms of the Gothic style, even in its seemingly most unfettered caprices, and to be observed as much as in the most formal conceptions of the Grecian school, cannot," he adds, "be denied, without letting Gothic art loose from all restraints which make it rational and true. But it is a law felt rather than understood, and the suggestions made respecting it must be offered with diffidence."

Thus far, the Reviewer can hardly fail to carry us with him. But he proceeds to inquire into the nature of proportion; and here, I think, plausible as his view is, we must suspend our judgment. This theory is thus stated and applied: "Proportion," he says, "by its very nature, is *the conformity of certain spaces and lengths to some one common measure*, either multiplied or repeated, or divided. But the mind can never become sensible of it except by referring admeasurements to some previously assumed standard, and observing their conformity to it, or their discrepancy. The first thing then to find in a Gothic, or indeed in any other building, is the line

or lines which are taken as the base, from which all
other admeasurements are calculated. The second, to
discover the principles on which this line itself was constructed, i. e. why it was made of a greater or less
length. The third, to investigate the laws which regulated the relations borne to it by all the other lines of
the building." He then adduces some optical or pictu-
resque reasons (somewhat fanciful and unscientific ones,
we fear,) why, in a church, *the half breadth of the nave*
would be the fittest unit of measure to be adopted in
arranging the entire plan. Here Mr Wallen comes most
opportunely to his aid, by shewing, from actual measurements, that this rule applies, as a matter of fact, for whatever reason, to a considerable number of churches and
cathedrals, in England and abroad. Thus the half-width
of Salisbury nave is 39 feet; length of nave $195 = 5 \times 39$;
choir $= 158 = (4 \times 39) + 2$; transept $= 117 = 3 \times 39$.
Width of *York* nave $= 53$; length $= 219 = (4 \times 53) + 7$.
And so on. The Reviewer thus sums up, p. 407: "That
such a theory, stated thus absolutely, can scarcely hold
good in all instances......is highly probable. It may be
sufficient to suggest this broadly, that a horizontal lateral
line of width calculated in all cases, but calculated differ-
ently under different circumstances, will be found probably
to supply the normal scale to which all the rest of the
building is subsequently adjusted. It is obvious also, that
if the other minute subdivisions of the building are to be
framed upon it, it must be a measure susceptible of certain
powers of division and multiplication; one which contains
within it adequate arithmetical properties and functions
for all the purposes to which it was to be subsequently
applied." This whole theory abounds in felicitous guesses,
particularly in laying down the canon, that the breadth-

line will influence the whole arrangements. As a whole, however, it proceeds upon an erroneous conception and definition of "proportion;" and, as a matter of fact, would be found not to hold in a vast number of instances. Even in these alleged, we see that it is not accurately, only approximately, true, that the half-breadth of the nave is a common measure of the other dimensions of the buildings. Neither is the "common measure" alleged, as e. g. 52, capable of the subdivisions above required. I shall account presently for the theory's holding so far as it does hold, and for its holding no further. At present I proceed to offer a more correct definition of proportion.

We have seen that the conception of proportion, which all writers and theorists on architecture, from Vitruvius downwards, have entertained, has been that it consisted in "*linear commensurability.*" Proportion, they tell us, *uno ore,* " consists in the conformity of spaces and lengths to one common measure." "Symmetry," says Vitruvius, "results from proportion, or analogia. It is the commensuration of the various parts with the whole." It is obvious to ask, what proof is there that proportion consists in this? But the point is assumed throughout. It is not difficult to see the origin of the mistake. It is not the first time that a whole theory has been built upon a false derivation. Some well-known instances occur in Aristotle and Herodotus, some account of which may be found in the History of the Inductive Sciences. And, in more modern times, it is not very uncommon to meet with theories of education, which are apparently built upon a false derivation of the word, as if it came from *educere,* " to draw forth the powers," &c., and not, as it really does, from *educare,* which signifies neither

more nor less than "to fatten swine or cattle." The false
derivation on which shipwreck has been made in the instance before us, is, as it would seem, that of the Greek
συμμετρία. It has been assumed to signify "commensurability." Now there is no doubt that Aristotle does use
σύμμετρος in this sense. He speaks of σύμμετρα μεγέθη,
and σύμμετροι ἀριθμοι, "magnitudes which have a common
measure ;" "numbers which have a common measure." He
calls the problem commonly known as "the squaring of the
circle," the question "whether the diameter is commensurable (σύμμετρος) with the circumference." But Constan-
tine justly observes (in voc.), that συμμετρία is a word
which may be variously understood, according to the
matter it refers to ; hence, when Aristotle uses it, as he
does in the Ethics, of a well-proportioned figure, (Eth. iv.
οἱ μικροὶ......σύμμετροι, καλοὶ δ' οὔ), there is no reason
for concluding that he builds his notion of symmetry or
proportion on commensurability. It seems absurd to
suppose that by calling a well-proportioned man σύμμετρος, he means that the length of his hand or foot was
a common measure of his other dimensions. There can
be no doubt that all that he meant was that his body
was so proportioned, that any alteration in the size or
disposition of the parts would diminish its beauty. His
using, however, a word which, strictly speaking, involves
the idea of actual measurement, shews that in his conception, or that of his native language, proportion is
properly *the result of systematic measurement of some kind
or other*. The only question is, what kind of measurement;
and how comes it to depend upon it ? That it is *not* commensurability, whether of lines or spaces, that produces
good proportion is manifest, since at that rate a pillar
100 feet high by 1 foot broad would be well-proportioned.

Nor can any reason be given why this condition should give pleasure to the eye. It supposes a very improbable process of mental arithmetic to be continually going forward, on view of any structure submitted to the eye. The Latin *proportio* (which, however, is never applied to architecture) has seemed to confirm, by its derivation, this mistake. What, then, is the συμμετρία of the Greeks? what is the *kind* of measurement which conduces, in their conception, to beauty of form, and specially in architecture? Now it has been well observed, (Penny Cycl. art. "Architecture,") that "the nation to which Europe is indebted for the elements of its architecture, is also that to which we owe those of *geometry*. That law of the mind which gave birth to the simple forms of the triangle, the circle, and the square, gave to man the elements of all his works of art. We do not know of any nation that has carried architecture to perfection, or even to a degree of excellence in its kind, which has not also had a system of geometry and arithmetic." The Egyptians, the Greeks, the Hindoos, and the mediæval Europeans, are all instances in point. The Egyptians, who erected temples for their many gods, also measured out and apportioned the land yearly, after the overflow of the Nile, *geometrically*[1]. The Greeks had their Thales and Euclid as well as their architects; the Indian his mathematics as well as his cases of Elephanta; and the Norman conquerors, who brought the "new style" (as William of Malmsbury calls it) into England, also surveyed it for Domesday Book. It is not unnatural to look for some connexion between these sciences, thus found inseparably hand-in-hand. In short, we can hardly doubt that *geometry* was

---

[1] On Egyptian geometry, v. Jomard, stâne metrique des anciens Egyptians: et cf. Herod. ii. 6.

at the bottom of the Greek, and all other right conceptions of *proportion*. Their συμμετρία, we must needs conjecture, must be a geometrical conception; συμμετρία must have reference to *harmonious geometrical measurement* of some kind. And if we inquire what " harmonious measurements " are, we cannot doubt that they are such as involve equidistances, and equiangularities. Such figures then as are referred to one centre, whether a point or a line, and form and crystallize about it, will be *symmetrical;* and pre-eminently, all regular figures inscribable in a circle. The former kind, viz. equidistant measurement from a central *line,* is the lowest and simplest notion of symmetry or proportion. It is under this conception, indeed, that " symmetry " has passed into our common language. We call anything symmetrical which admits of a line being drawn through it, which shall divide it into a series of equidistances; the human figure, e. g. But the symmetry of regular figures, i. e. of figures inscribable in a circle, is something more than this. It is also singularly beautiful, as combining the comprehension and regularity of the circle with vivacity and decision of the rectilineal and angular outline.

Such then being geometrical harmony or συμμετρία, the hypothesis is, that the Greeks and others who have excelled in architecture, made it the basis of their architectural proportion: that it was hence that the Greeks applied the term *symmetria* to good proportion in architecture. In another work published by Mr Griffith, entitled, " Suggestions for developing the Temples of Greece, by Geometrical Proportions," he has shewn that those buildings actually were constructed on the basis of regular geometrical figures. And I need hardly advert to the fact that he has triumphantly proved the same of at least many of the finest specimens of Gothic architecture. The geometrical principle which he has established in relation to the latter, may be more fully enunciated than it has been by himself, in the following canon: "*That the revolution of regular figures, and of the equilateral triangle especially, on their axis, into positions of alternation, regulates, by the position and intersections of them, the proportions and arrangement of the building and its accessories.*" A glance at any of the figures here drawn out will sufficiently verify the canon. It will be seen that the width of the building generally furnishes the basis of the regulating equilateral triangle: this affords confirmation, up to a certain point, of the ingenious observations and guesses of Mr Wallen and the Reviewer. Moreover, the linear proportions which Mr Wallen has shewn to exist between the width and the length of certain churches, are accounted for by the fact of those churches having been constructed on the equi-laterali-triangular basis. For so it is, that half the base of an equilateral triangle is very nearly, though not exactly, commensurable with some of the longitudinal measurements obtained by setting out the triangles in Mr Griffith's manner. This then is the reason why the length of Salisbury nave is found to be five times its half-width; the length of York nave, seven feet more than eight times its half-width; and so on. These positions are true as a matter of fact; but it is not true that the architects consciously worked on this plan; it is an accident of their plan, not the principle of it. The reason why Vitruvius found,—if he did find,— a certain linear relation between the dimensions of the parts in Grecian architecture, was because geometrical rules, accidentally involving such relations, were employed in the construction. And we do not hesitate to set down the "common measure" of the whole building, proposed by Mr Wallen and the Reviewer, viz., the *half*-width line, as fanciful and erroneous.

But we have still to inquire, why it is that buildings planned upon a geometrical basis afford pleasure to the eye. All that we have done hitherto is to establish, on etymological and other grounds, the probability of a connection between geometry and the buildings, whether of Greece or the middle ages, which thus affect the eye. It is not a sufficient account of the matter to say that there is geometrical regularity, and that this has a kind of harmony about it, and gives pleasure to the eye, as being referable to a centre: this is one element, no doubt, in the pleasurable impression given; but it is not the whole; else a square or a pentagon, a cube or a pyramid, taken nakedly as they are in themselves, would be certain of being pleasing forms to build in; but we do not find them to be so, nor are they, in this form, adopted by the masters of the art. There is a selection exercised by them: it is not *all* kinds of geometrical regularity, but certain kinds and combinations of it, as we have seen, that they work upon. When we understand the grounds of this selection, we have mastered the secret of their wonderful buildings, and in short, the secret of PROPORTION itself. Now what other principle can it be, we would ask, than an *optical* one? In speaking of proportion in buildings, we speak not of a thing conceived and held in the mind, as ratios or the like, nor yet of a thing mapped out on a sheet of paper, as a mathematical diagram, but of a thing which forms a view, or picture, so to speak, before the eyes: this is more especially true of the interior proportion. Our "Proportion," that is, is not conceptional, nor mathematical, but *optical*. Can we, then, the next question is, can we detect in the selection as to kinds of geometrical regularity, made both by the Grecian and mediæval architects, any symptoms of a reference and conformity to optical laws? I venture to say that such may be discovered. And while I offer the following remarks with diffidence, I at the same time request particular attention to them, as aiming, successfully or not, at the root of the whole matter: a further investigation of so interesting a subject is much to be desired.

I must again request your attention to some diagrams. It is a traditional rule, commonly received among architects and builders, that the interior of a room is well-proportioned, *if the length of the side equals the diagonal of the square of their end.* No. 8. exhibits a ground-plan thus proportioned. BE is the diagonal of the square formed upon the end AB; and the side BD is equal to BE. Now supposing this to be true, that a room thus proportioned does give pleasure to the eye, (and I find that the proportion holds of some remarkable ancient buildings; as the Maison Carrée, at Nismes, and, what is curious, *the chancel of the Temple Church*), I conceive the reason of it to be this: that the eye takes a pleasure—for some reason or other, of which hereafter—in imagining the revolution of a principal line, such as the diameter of this square (which it instinctively forms for itself) into another principal position. And this optical reason may be given for its taking such pleasure. It is well known that in the mechanism of the eye there is a telescopic contrivance by which it adjusts itself for the purpose of viewing nearer or more distant objects. If we are looking at an object within a few inches of the eye, we do not see distinctly the more distant objects within the range of vision; and on attempting to do so we are conscious of a

change in the adjustment of the eye. Moreover this
change is rather disagreeable than otherwise, from its
causing a dazzled sensation; as any one may convince
himself by trying the experiment on a very near and
very distant object. Hence it will follow, that the eye, in
reviewing any scene presented to it, which it cannot see all
at once, will be agreeably affected by points of equidistance,
because it can view them without any unpleasant change
in its telescopic action. Thus on entering a room proportioned as above, at one corner of it, the area is for the
most part spanned without an effort, the eye revolving
through the arc ED. And this I take to be the funda-
mental principle of proportion in architecture. Indeed,
it is apparently one reason why the vault of the heavens
affords pleasure to the eye, that it perfectly answers this
condition of equidistance.

Let us now proceed to apply this primary principle to
Grecian and Gothic architecture. I would first request
attention, however, to the process which the eye, according to our hypothesis, performs on the simple specimen
of proportion here submitted to it. It first forms a square
for itself on the end of the room, or cuts off such square
from the whole length of it; then takes the diagonal of
this, and conceives it as revolving into a new position.
That is to say, it satisfies itself in the first instance with
the contemplation of a symmetrical geometrical form, and,
secondarily, selects and combines certain of its elements
in accordance with an optical law. A twofold source of
pleasure to the eye is therefore to be here recognised.
Passing on to Greek architecture, we detect a very curious
and even astonishing confirmation of this view of the
sources of " proportion." No. 9. exhibits the façade of the
Temple of Theseus at Athens, drawn in such a manner as

to exhibit its geometrical construction, according to Mr Griffith. AB is the entire width of the Temple. The width of four out of the six columns (whose position is fixed by a method to be explained presently) being taken as a base (AG), and a square (ADHG) erected upon it, this decides the height of the entablature, or of the façade. If now the distance AB, i.e. the entire width, be taken in the compasses, and the pencil leg placed at D, while the other finds a centre C for itself on the central perpendicular line CE, and then the arc DF be described cutting the central perpendicular in F, *this will decide, in all cases, the height and angle of the pediment.* Now there is nothing more puzzling or unaccountable to our Gothic notions than the pitch of the Grecian pediments. We admit their harmony in their places; but they have hitherto seemed to defy all conceivable rules. I do say therefore that a discovery like this—for I do not hesitate to call it such—of the principle of their construction is very remarkable. Let us now take notice of the principle of it. And I say that the principle is identically the same as that which we have seen in a well-proportioned room; only that this is a more complex instance. The eye first forms for itself a square, i.e. a symmetrical figure. Then taking the line of breadth, and applying it in a particular manner, viz. so as to reach from the *diagonal point* D to the central perpendicular, it conceives it to revolve into the vertical position, thus deciding the great question of all, the entire height, and the pitch of the pediment, as before it decided in a similar way the great question, the length of the room. The difference between the two cases is, that instead of the diagonal of the square being allowed to revolve on its own angle, another line is placed *in a position regulated by the diagonal.*

Herein, then, would appear to lie the secret of that majestic and indescribable repose, which all ages have agreed to recognise in the Temples of Greece. Mr Griffith has applied this to six of the Grecian temples in his published work; viz. besides this one of Theseus, that of Themis at Rhamnus, the Parthenon, the Ionic temple on the Ilissus, that of Erechtheus at Athens, and of Bacchus at Teos. He also enters into many details which are geometrically decided. Proceeding to Gothic architecture, we have only to refer to the geometrically-constructed plans before us, in order to perceive that here also beauty of proportion is referable to the same optical considerations. For what was our canon above enunciated? " That *the revolution of regular figures into certain positions* regulates the proportions and arrangment of the building." Here then, as in the cases already alleged, the eye forms to itself a symmetrical figure, and conceives certain elements in it, viz. all its sides, to revolve into certain other positions. This is the simplest account of the matter. It is also here, as in the two former instances, the *line of breadth* that by its revolution into those positions generates the scheme of the building. But it is obvious that much more than this enters in to make up the Gothic phase of architectural proportion. In the first place, the new positions taken up by the lines after their revolution, are positions of symmetrical alternation with the original ones: this holds equally of those buildings in which the square is the geometrical basis, as of the others. But in the much more common case, where the equilateral triangle is the basis, an additional consideration, and that an optical one, would seem to enter in to complete the harmony of impression conveyed by the building. It is a well-known optical law, that an object is then most perfectly seen when the rays which enter the eye from its extremities make an angle of 60° with each other. Now the triangle being equilateral, each of its angles *is* of 60°. To an eye, therefore, placed at any of the angular points, all the objects lying in the lines of the containing sides, or intervening between them, will be distinctly seen. And a glance at the diagrams, e. g. of the Temple, or Maplestead, will shew that, by the arrangement adopted, as many principal points and objects as possible (as windows, pillars, openings, &c.) are made to lie upon these lines. This principle of arranging as many principal points as possible òn certain main lines of vision was not unknown to the Greek architects. No. 10. is a ground-plan of the Temple of Theseus, whose elevation we have already noticed. The outer parallelogram is that of the *peristyle*, the inner one, that of the *cella*. Two isosceles triangles, raised on the end lines as a base, decide, by their intersection, the position of the side walls of the cella. To an eye at C all the main points of the arrangement appear along the external and intermediate lines of vision; along the first or external pair of lines are seen the centre of the cella walls, and the two outer pillars of the hexastyle portico; along the second pair, the extremities of the cella walls, and the second pair of pillars of the portico; along the third or middle pair, the aperture of the cella door, the single pair of pillars belonging to the cella, and the central pair of portico pillars. This therefore is a very remarkable confirmation of the principle of arrangment we seem to detect in our Gothic specimens. The refinement of making the lines of vision to contain 60° is due to the Gothic architects. (See however the Temple of Bacchus, sup.).

It only remains to notice one or two objections which

may be made to Mr Griffith's geometrical scheme, or to the explanations here attempted of the principles involved in it. The absence of documentary evidence may be alleged against the entire scheme. This is at best a negative objection. However, so it is, that documentary evidence is not wanting in indirect confirmation of Mr Griffith's views. His method of planning out the Round Church with alternating squares has been adopted by an ingenious friend of the writer to decide the plan and proportions on which octagonal and circular pillars in Norman Churches were constructed : thus applying the principle to details. Now though we have as yet discovered no document which expressly refers Gothic *ground-plans* to such a principle, yet a paper of the 14th century has been found and lately published in the Archæological Journal, in which directions on exactly this principle are given for proportioning a *pinnacle* : which is enough to affirm the principle historically. As to our own view, connecting this scheme with optical considerations, it may be said, that the eye is not actually, or but seldom, placed in the angular position from which alone it can realize the view on which we have supposed "proportion" to depend. I answer, that the hypothesis on this point is, that the eye *conceives itself* so placed, and by habit judges whether a building is so arranged as to possess such points of view. Again, it may be objected, that our professed well-proportioned building, is, after all, only a succession of well-proportioned parts,—the successive bays, for instance, of the nave. This is admitted : and it is conceived that the number of such successive parts, and therefore the length of the entire building, was a much more arbitrary matter than the proportioning and arrangement of the several units, so to speak, of which it consisted. The defect, if it be one, is shared by the Grecian temples, which are very nearly of the same height, though varying in width from four to eight or more columns : the square, which is the unit, in their case, being repeated almost at pleasure, just as in Gothic the triangular unit is re- peated along the length of the building. Only there the pediment, bearing a fixed relation to the whole breadth, comes in to harmonize the whole ; and it may be that future researches will bring to light some principles of pyramidal arrangement or the like, which shall account for the number of times that the unit is repeated in Gothic, and settle other points which we have yet to comprehend in the marvellous structures of the middle ages of Europe. It may be objected, again, to the theory of Proportion here advanced, that it is too purely phy- sical. Instead of recognizing a standard of beauty im- planted in us, conformity to which constitutes good pro- portion, it refers us to the organic structure of the eye, and the pleasurable sensations arising from its unimpeded action, as the source of proportion in architecture. The former view is that of the Platonic philosophy. The latter, which is here adopted, finds a most complete ana- logy in the science of music. According to the received theory, " whenever the exciting cause of sound is one, the vibrations of which can be shewn to be performed in ex- actly the same time, so that the waves caused by them are all of the same length, we perceive a sound which gives pleasure to the ear, and has the name of *harmonious* or *musical*. In other words, we may consider it as certain, that *the pleasure arising from musical sounds is a consequence of the perfectly equal times of the vibrations which produce them*, and of its result, the equal lengths of the sonorous waves propagated from them through the atmosphere." Moreover "it is found by experiment that two sounds are more or less *consonant*, when heard together, according as the relation between their vibrations is more or less simple. Thus, when two vibrations of the first are made in one vibration of the second, (which is the simplest ratio possible) that similarity of sounds is observed, which is so close that we call them both the same sound, only the one an octave higher than the other." That is to say, the physical constitution of the ear is such, that it takes notice when the times of the waves which impel it are equal, and derives pleasure from such notice. Again, it takes notice when the ratio which the waves of two sounds bear to each other is simple and uninvolved, and takes pleasure from this notice likewise, even to the extent of pronouncing such sounds admissible simultaneously. And the reason of this pleasure would seem to be, because there is equability, calmness, freedom from irregularity and distraction, about the appulsion of waves of sound under these conditions. Therefore it is no less true than beautiful, which has been said, that "music is *the consolation of the ear*[1]." And if music is the consolation of the ear, why may not Proportion be "the repose of the eye"? And such our theory makes it to be. It represents the eye as feeling satisfaction in such observations as are painless, effortless and complete.

It would be impossible to conclude this paper without some allusion, however brief, to the subject of freemasonry, and the symbolical, that is, in fact, the *religious* aspect of the theory we have been investigating. As to the freemasons,—if I remember aright,—the square, the circle,

[1] Jer. Taylor.

and the triangle, figure among the traditionary symbols of
that effete fraternity. Can anything be more probable,
than that the importance which they now attach to them,
without knowing why, originated in the fact which we
have been engaged in considering, viz. the undoubted use
of these figures as the basis of architectural construction
by the ancient masons? But more deeply interesting still
is the symbolical aspect of the subject. If we admit,—as
I think we can hardly refuse to do,—the correctness of
Mr Griffith's beautiful theory of construction,—then did
the Gothic architects embody a religion and express a
faith, in the forms which they selected as the basis of their
sacred edifices, viz. the *equilateral triangle inscribed within
the circle;*—symbols of the Ever-Blessed Co-Equal Co-
Eternal Trinity in Unity. But if, further, there be any
truth in the theory of Proportion, which it has been the
object of this paper to ground on the observation of these
facts; if architects COULD NOT build otherwise, to produce
harmonious and perfect structures, than on the basis of
these same figures, then do we attain to a deeper and more
wonderful truth still. It has been well observed by that
excellent divine and musician, Jones of Nayland, that
"man may invent musical sounds, but the principles of
harmony are in the elements of nature." The great law
of the sevenfold harmony is written for him in the constitution of the " wind that bloweth where it listeth:" so
that he cannot look into the mystery of his own power of
producing harmonious sound, without being reminded, in
a startling manner, of the sevenfold operation of that Spirit
by which chaos was at the first "gathered into order."
And even so, when we take in hand to inquire what it is
that enables man to lend something like perfection to the

least perishable and most sacred of the works of his hands, we find that into the laws of vision, upon which these results are founded, is inseparably interwoven the conception of the Co-Equal, the Triune, and the Eternal.

--------

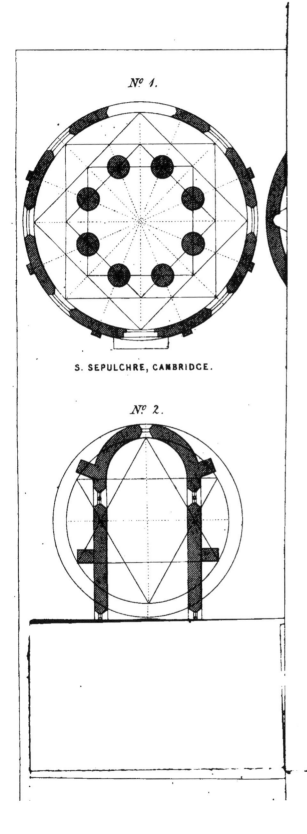

N.º 1.

S. SEPULCHRE, CAMBRIDGE.

N.º 2.

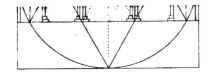

CHANCEL OF TEMPLE CHURCH.

Nº 6.

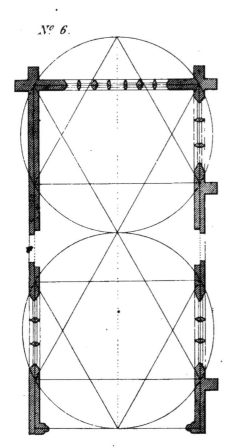

CHANCEL, HAWTON, NOTTS.